Join Me

For

Tea

A Special Brew: 1 Tsp of Transparency, 9 Slices of Wisdom & 1 Tsp of Courage

ROXANNE REID

DayeLight

PUBLISHERS

ISBN: 978-1-953759-15-3

I dedicate this book to my nine-year-old self. It was at that moment that I first learnt, word for word, Kirk Franklin's song "My Life Is In Your Hands."

Join Me

For

Tea

A Special Brew: 1 Tsp of Transparency, 9 Slices of Wisdom & 1 Tsp of Courage

Acknowledgments

I must pause to acknowledge, not a person, as it is commonly done, but the setbacks and major disappointments in my life. Without these obstacles, I would have no conflict upon which to build the plot of my life. So whole-heartedly, though unusual: thank you doubt; when I became tired of you, I had no other choice but to believe in myself.

Thank you fear. You were the biggest monster of them all, but I slew you. I wrote the book.

Thank you delayed gratification: when I realize that I could not pound my fist on your wall for too long, I learned patience. It was in this moment of waiting and reflecting that I decided to write this book.

Finally, thank you failed relationships of all sorts. You taught me that I was the problem, for I deserved more, but I did not know. That led me to get in touch with who I really am. Now that I know myself, it is such a beauty.

Join Me

For

Tea

A Special Brew: 1 Tsp of Transparency, 9 Slices of Wisdom & 1 Tsp of Courage

Table of Contents

Join Me

For

Tea

A Special Brew: 1 Tsp of Transparency, 9 Slices of Wisdom & 1 Tsp of Courage

Introduction

I wrote this book for you, yes you. I am sharing my life's story with people everywhere. If you have had a difficult emotional childhood, whether things happened to you or you initiated these challenges, welcome to my story. In a world that sells perfection, it has now become taboo to remove the masks of being perfect in order to share the blisters and scars we were told to hide.

This story is the unmasking of my "perfect," to show to all my personal challenges and ugly scars with the hope that you too will be encouraged to be truthful to yourself. Let me dwell here for a while. I want you to understand that it is absolutely okay to be honest with yourself; you can pretend with people, close and far, but how long do you think you can lie to your own self? Soon enough, your soul's truth will demand of you its truth. What then will you do? Whether you, like me, a millennial, who chooses to look at the bigger picture of humanity or you believe you must take the puzzle of this great vastness called life and look at the pieces—piece by piece—you are certainly not alone. Whatever you do in this life or the next, do so valiantly and remember to be good to yourself. Be good to yourself, my people. Be good to you.

Join Me

For

Tea

A Special Brew: 1 Tsp of Transparency, 9 Slices of Wisdom & 1 Tsp of Courage

Chapter One: Love Brew

On Matters of Love

*I*t took me some time to understand how God could be classified as "Love." I just never understood how the two words could be joined in one sentence. When God was shoved unto me as a young girl, in my eyes, the people who knew God were odd: they never smiled or laughed; they did not seem alive. One evening, I overheard someone who "really knew" God told someone else who did not that there were two things God would never do: one was that God would never send a husband back to his wife. God simply will not do it.

Something turned deep down inside of me, and you know those moments when you feel an odd low "uh-oh" feeling? That was how I felt. I surmised that God really was an old man, far away in the sky, and He was very bossy, could not be pleased unless you did exactly as

He said, the minute He said it and, finally, God was too high above comforting a wife whose husband walked out on her by helping him to find his way back. I lost touch with God because surely the person who gave those instructions knew God, and I had never seen her with a partner, ever.

So, there I was, lost in confusion, swimming through life's chaos without the wisdom that God is in every little breath we take, every little giggle made, every little beat of the heart, and every little fond memory of loved ones. For want of a better word, this "softness" of God was hidden for twenty-nine years and some change. I found solace hearing the beautiful testimonies of single women who boasted that God wrote their love stories on several blogs, and some even described how God helped to select their wedding dresses. I was floored, like, which "God" did that? Is God really THAT personal with us? Oh my! I felt warmth when men and women of the cloth boldly confessed how God helped them see the best in their spouses and work towards a healthy and happy married life. That was new to me, but it radically changed my perception of God in matters of love.

We often forget, and some of us really did not and still do not know who God is. It was marvelous when I began to discover that the estranged woman I pass so often on the road begging had some trace of God in her. The little boy selling mangoes on the corner to help his family so that he could be present at school only on Mondays and Thursdays had some trace of God within, and so did his family. The newborn, so helpless and defenseless, carry the same, if not a stronger trace of God within but, so often, we lose our sense of 'sensitivity' that we lose the God within us; the God who is and can only be love.

Now, some persons may be worried at this point since most of us have had our fair share (even more than this) of manipulation and abuse by significant others, family, so-called friends, colleagues, etc. We have seen those who stood for love, and those who preached love, killed or tortured. There is no going around this. It happens. However, scripture states that perfect love casts out all fear, and in this context of love, this also means wisdom. Proverbs 1:20-23 says, "Wisdom cries out in the street; in the squares she raises her voice. At the busiest corner she cries out; at the entrance of the city gates she speaks: 'How long, O simple ones, will you love being simple? How long will scoffers delight in their scoffing and fools hate knowledge? Give heed to my reproof; I will pour out my thoughts to you; I will make my words known to you." (NRSVA).

Here, what stood out to me is that wisdom is presented as the feminine essence that spills over into discernment. Notice the locations that wisdom kept busy on: the streets, in squares, corners, and entrances to cities. Could this suggest that:

1. There is much to be considered from the common/simple things, should we take a second look at the simplest of ideas, people, etc.?

2. Are there things/ideas hidden in plain sight that can make our life's journey a lot easier?

3. Are we simple-minded people? If we are, when/where did we lose our depth? When were we taught to forget our intuition and insight of ourselves and others?

4. Could it be concluded that more of us have lost insight than those who heard and followed the instructions of being wise? If this is the case, are those who we follow, whether on social media or as mentors, wise, and how could we possibly know?

5. What in the world is wisdom? (Definition in the next chapter).

Am I suggesting that those who taught love and were put to death were unwise/foolish? Absolutely not. I am putting forward that if most of us realize that love walks hand in hand with wisdom, then greatness could possibly ooze from all over the world. Galatians 5:22-23 speaks about the nine fruits of the Spirit: "But the *fruit of the Spirit* is love, joy, peace, forbearance, kindness, goodness, faithfulness, gentleness and self-control" (NIV), but where is wisdom? I believe that if we look closely at these nine fruits, we could surmise that the tree that bears all these fruits is wisdom.

And now, what of true love?

Well, this, I believe, is the unquenchable respect, grace, and mercy that we hold ourselves by, for ourselves firstly, then, to those who share the same spark. I know, this is not the answer you were looking forward to hearing, but let's face the music; too many times have I searched for a supposed love that "gets" me, one that sweeps me off my feet and makes my life perfect. Who would not require a love like this, especially when it is branded as "true?"

I withdrew from the dating scene for three years and counting, after making horrendous mistakes, one after the other, and I had an epiphany. Imagine that! I was my own best friend and lover, if you will, but I did not die, nor was I desperate. I was forced to take the forever vow, "In sickness and in health, for better or for worst, for richer or for poorer, 'til death us do part…'" with, well, myself. With a poker face, I will admit that as I said those words to no one but myself, I felt frightened since I did not know what lay ahead for me or what my story was to begin with.

How could I commit to myself? I was taught to look for someone "better" with whom I would be complete. I thought it was only then do we take that type of serious vow. However, I took it knowing so well that I was conscious now that I was fully responsible for my life, actions, decisions, behaviour, and response to people, whether they treated me badly or with respect. I finally found solace in myself. These words, "til death us do part" woke up a sleeping giant deep within the caves of my immortal spirit, so much so that my entire body quivered as I responded to myself, "I do." My consciousness shifted from dependency or searching for a "fix" in circumstances or people, especially those looking for the same fix I was, into that of dignity and self-awareness. I became my own happily ever after. I was my own best friend ever. I was my sole confidant, and my royal diaries/journal entries kept a score of my many vivid dreams and daily ideas. I knew that I was not the same person. I became confident as a woman, a girl, and as a student of life in this realm. What others would gladly see as weird, I saw as an opportunity that even the blind could see; that it afforded me a chance to get to know, court, and fall madly in love with myself. I finally found the "I" in me, truly, Roxanne Reid.

Now, imagine, dear ones, if each of us took up this same mantle to pull away and get to know who we really are. Imagine the fireworks as you listen to the love languages of your soul. Imagine, as with each heartbeat, it heals you of past failures and pain of who you thought you were. Imagine what this self-discovery could do to a random child, born impoverished with no true role model. Love is not a mystery after all. It cannot be stressed enough, and is no mistake that the entry of this book began with establishing love. Before we give or expect to receive love at its truest, safest, most healthy form, we first must clean our house; our houses must be without spot or wrinkle. Such a great sacrifice because it takes time, but once it is completed, it must, has to, attract a love that recognizes its true partner. If you truly want to experience true love, start looking within. Clean your house spotlessly. Wash the windows of your soul. Scrub the floors of your roots. Discover the open doors of your ancestry. Wash the garments of your purpose. Stand before the mirror of your truth. Be confident in who you are. Love will and must come to those who are prepared.

15

Message to My Inner Child

Baby, you are loved. Even if/when you wreck your own life; even if/when you did or are still doing some things that you know deep down you should not even have to stoop that low. Even if/when you are going around in circles right at this moment; Even if/when you do not know who you are and you cannot identify your gifts or talents; Even if you are classified as a third world or first world country citizen, whether you were born in the slums or the wealthiest neighbourhoods, whether you can read this or you had someone read to you, listen clearly, you are loved.

Yes, God loves us. God loves you. But I want you to know that God lives within us, so God/Love is within us, and no matter what it seems like right now or what you may even believe, there is still a trace of God/Love in you, and you are perfectly loved in your imperfect state.

I want you to know that when no one is near and, on those days, when there is no one to call, you are still loved, and help is on the way to you. Always.

You may feel defenseless. You may have been abused: verbally, sexually, spiritually, financially, physically, or psychologically. But, wipe your tears, baby. You. Are. Not. Alone.

Do you hear me?

You. Are. Not. Alone, and have never been. I am here with you, and together with God, we will figure this thing out. Not only that, we will thrive.

Signed _____   Date _____

Poem: Hearts on Fire

Hearts on Fire
Blazing bright
Where love is tender
And sorrows are light
Dreams are touched
Pain forgotten
Guilt released
Abuse-corrected
Acceptance comes wrapped in a gift box
Jealousy channeled into goodwill
Envy into dedication
Death and gloom are mixed together
And placed in the sun to bleach
The sting of death, now forgotten
I stand unafraid
Walking directly towards the Light
Taking it from the bearer's hand and stepping out in faith
In a world where darkness seems to get a bad rap
While men worship the presence of the Light
Is there not beauty in things unseen?
And aren't things unseen in darkness lies?
What if light was dark
And dark was light?
With what would our souls now rejoice?
Can the mediation between darkness and light be—Love?

Poem: Hearts on Fire

Unconditional.
Over all.

Hearts on Fire
Acceptance lingers
Communities strengthened
Peace runs with speed in the streets
Men and women share the bliss
With children
Share the bliss
With the forgotten
Share the bliss
With those in mental prisons
Share the bliss with all God's children
And now the Earth sings
The ocean joins in with fine dance
The Wind blows sweetly, giving the beat
Fire gives its light and its heat
Its warmth.
Hearts' on Fire

Chapter Two: Wisdom Brew

On Matters of Wisdom

*F*or twenty-nine years and some change, I did not understand what it meant to be wise. Through the eyes of a nine-year-old child, I observed my surroundings, learned about simple cause and effect situations and, of course, action and consequences. Wisdom, then, meant staying obedient, getting good grades, and being good. Nothing off there, except, I cannot remember being wise as only a child can be, nor have I thought of myself as wise as I grew. I simply stayed out of trouble and followed a straight path to, what...? Ah! An education and what a great accomplishment this was for me at twenty-five. I had a first degree (thanks, mommy), but I did not, not even once, implored my mind on whether I was wise or otherwise.

Children cannot help but cling to and love their parents, no matter who or what these people are. A child's love will see through it all and still have nothing but pure love for his/her parents. For several years, under covers unbeknownst to anyone, I cried to stem the pain of my physically and emotionally absent father. I could not understand how I were to function as a whole person without a father. So, each flaw that others pointed out in my physical appearance, psychological wellbeing, etc., and those I found in myself, I linked with the thought that, well, it must be because I was different. My father did not provide for me, protect me, or offered me his hand to hold or his arms to cushion me, so how could I expect to be secure? This went on for a long time, until these ideas turned into beliefs that I had accepted. Where am I going with this? Stay with me.

So here I was as a child and throughout my teens and early adulthood, still that fearful, timid, anxious nine-year-old who cried non-stop under the covers for her father and unconditional love. When so-called friends or relatives began to intimidate me, I would shrink back because then I thought they had the right to. Who was I to defend myself against those who must know what was right for me and those who had both parents present?

Then, one day, something turned. I wrote a story about a lost puppy for a class assignment, and we all lined up so that our teacher could mark our books. I was freaking out because most classmates were getting quick slaps in their palm with a ruler. When it was my turn, my teacher had to take the book from my hand that was now at my side, limping. I was fearful that I was not and would never ever be the one to escape that proper flogging; after all, what could I write? She took my book, and I half-watched, half looked down on my shoes. She was real quiet until she began chuckling; I mean good chuckling, and when her eyes met mine, she had water in them. She said to me, "Pickney, yu really can write story enu and to how you look, like you expect flogging, mi know yu nu confident." With softer eyes, she asked, "Where is your confidence, Roxanne?"

I walked away with a fire in my heart, determined that if my grade six teacher said I could write and my story was excellent, I would hold my head a little higher from then on, even if I felt like I was less than, or almost good enough.

So, how does this experience relate to one being wise? Experience has taught me that the starting point of wisdom is not being a slave to my feelings. My feelings told me that since my father did not love me, my life would be nothing to be proud about; nothing major. The moment I acknowledged how I felt and sorted them, literally placing them in categories and then eliminating the need to act on those that accused me of that which I had no control over, while acting on those that brought more happiness, balance, comfort and compassion to myself, I began to feel whole.

Wisdom, at least the starting point as this topic is extensive, suggests that I can only control what goes on within me, not what happened before my existence, not what others do or say; what truly matters is how I choose to speak to myself, the thoughts I tell myself and how I treat myself. I believe strongly that wisdom is synonymous with the self-acceptance that comes by knowing who we are and what we came here to do.

So many of us have heard, "There's only one you," but how many of us have meditated on the possibilities of meanings brought forward? In my estimation, if there is only one you/me, it firstly brings forward that "I am" *or* "you are" *the one* actively perceiving everyone else and not the other way around. This idea opens up a can of worms because it makes one think about his/her daily occurrences with 'others' with a new perception that who/what "You" or "I" are experiencing is nothing but an extension of "You" or "I." Heavy stuff, and I can understand the side-eyes as some of us have had some unfortunate relations with those closest to us and "We" are nothing like "Them," right? In essence, "We" are indeed like "Them," but one of the differences may be that we chose to flan the flame within and share it, especially with those who are undeserving.

Wisdom, in my estimation, being synonymous with self-acceptance suggests here that sharing the light within us also runs over into holding this light close to us so that those without it cannot take it all or, worse, seek to put it out for their benefit. When we know who we are and what our gifts/talents are, wisdom speaks to us to remind us that treating ourselves first with fairness and then creating healthy boundaries may create a ripple effect for those who are not there yet, to get there.

Wisdom Tree Bears Fruit of the Spirit

Imagine a fruit tree. Use your imagination. Close your eyes and just do it. I am serious, do it! Now, for your tree, imagine different types of fruits on just one tree. Super tree! Can you imagine planting that one tree in your backyard? A tree that has all those fruits in one setting? Even if all fruits do not bear at once, that one tree has the potential and bears all fruits in different seasons.

This is purely my imagination. Wisdom is that tree. The nine fruits of the Spirit all grow on the Tree of Wisdom. When Love bears, Peace is resting until it is time for her blossoms to bud. After Love has given her fruit, she rests; she does not complain about Self-Control bearing three times this year. Wisdom starts within you and me, and she reminds us that a house divided against itself cannot stand.

How can one person display all nine fruit of the Spirit; is it reasonable? I believe that each of us has possible impossibilities that are untapped, so what is it to learn patience, learn to love God and each other, learn to have compassion, etc.? Patience is a necessary practice; there is just something about delayed gratification that teaches self-control, but patience alone cannot suffice for three hundred and sixty-five days for the rest of our lives. Variety is the spice of life, yes? And that is why many of us have a varied meal diet, which makes eating the same meal for an entire week unheard of. If someone suggests this as some sort of challenge, for example, "Let's start an oatmeal ONLY 2 weeks diet for weight loss," I would not want to see the look on some faces on the third night, having the third bowl of oats for the day. Do not get me started on Friday nights. You get the point.

Since variety is the spice of life, why then are we such creatures of habit, doing the same thing repeatedly but expecting a different result? Could this be why wisdom screams in the squares and raises her voice in the streets?

If my theory holds weight, wisdom is the full acceptance of self (knowing the "self" of who we are at the core), and since wisdom has to scream to get us to listen to her, it is safe to assume that somewhere, along our paths, we lost our "muchness." We prefer to be fed. We like instant food and the like. Goodness, we enjoy a great motivation. There is no problem to hastily form relationships of all sorts too, just to feel like we are not alone. So, one possible problem is that a few persons who have done their life's homework, garnered from experiences, have now poured into us all that they know; we are now addicted to this, so we tend to flock wherever there is a gathering "Squares" to get something.

We all need teachers like Ms. Brown, who asked, "Where is your confidence?" I will ask you, "Where is your 'muchness'?"

"Be wise as Serpents..."

Wait, are we not informed that the Christian world is suffering because of a snake to begin with? Well, Christ saw the essential need to remind His disciples to be wise as serpents.

Wisdom means trusting one's intuition, so discernment is not cast off as being paronoid.

Wisdom means understanding and accepting oneself so one can identify his/her core values in someone else as well as the absence of the same in others and then decide to remain true to his/herself.

Simply put, wisdom is learning the rules of any game and justly applying to become victorious. By extension, wisdom may pour over into learning the rules for the said game and creating a different game using said rules or changing the rules for the same game.

Wisdom is not manipulation, and it is not acting in an unkind, sinister manner. It is learning how, why, when, where, etc. and finding out how to execute in a fairly easier manner that preserves the light within yourself while fanning the flame of those nearby, without extinguishing yours.

By now, you would have gotten the point that "being harmless as doves" is not, absolutely not, synonymous with sitting in abuse or worst, being harmless as doves do not give you permission to train your mind to believe that you deserve any sort of abuse from anyone.

Being harmless as doves should fit "being wise as snakes" like a hand in a glove.

Message To My Inner Child

You are loved because wisdom praises you. Wisdom knows what you carry. Your gifts and talents are not the same as anyone else's. Even if others exhibit talent that you possess, when you are in your element, doing what only you can do, no one else can do what YOU were made to do. I am so sorry, baby, that all these years we suffered, and I allowed you to be bullied and abused because I lacked sacred wisdom.

24

Not anymore. No more accepting less than. No more abuse from anyone, even closest friends, spouses or families; everyone hurting us has to go!

We have heard the call for wisdom, and we are dedicating our lives to continue listening, learning, and following the path that only wisdom has walked, until we run and until we fly. Let's do this. Wisdom's got us. Wisdom has you covered.

Signed _____   Date _____

Join Me

For

Tea

A Special Brew: 1 Tsp of Transparency, 9 Slices of Wisdom & 1 Tsp of Courage

Poem: Wisdom Brew - If

If God had a wife, yes, a wife!
I said, if God had a wife,
Her name would be Wisdom
She would be God's peace, safety, and trust
God's heart would rest in Her
He would know no other
For there is none.
Wisdom would beckon to all her children
And call each of us Hers
Call each of us Children of God
Wisdom would be full of grace
A woman in fine style and nothing shy of class
She would nurture us in our dark spaces
And gently wipe waters from our faces
She would hug us, engulfing us in a huge grizzly bear hug
She would remember no wrongs
She would sit with us, take our wounds, and sing us a bedtime story
As she cleans,
As she heals us.
She would pray for us
And tell us "baby, you're short of nothing"

If God had a wife,
I'd call her Wisdom
Gentleness becomes her

Love rests within her
Fierce protection and careful correction are her hands and feet
Her head shines with the electrifying light of the Most High
And her smile carries the brightest watt
Her face is warm and flexible,
For she is alive, really.

If God truly had a wife
She was risen as well.
She's not dead.
If God had a wife.

Chapter Three: Healing Brew

On Matters of Healing Part 1

*W*hat a beautiful word: "Healing."

For twenty-nine years, healing never dawned on me. I did not know what it was. I did not know how to get it. I did not even know it was necessary for anything.

Growing up, and by observing different mediums (school, families, television), I soaked up how to tolerate something/someone, even if he/she/it is bad for me; kept a list of the bad he/she/it has done to me and then boom! Blow up! I was taught not so much to forgive anyone; I was taught never to forget what was done. In the same breath, I was taught how to look the other way or how to sweep dirt under the rug.

So, I never grew into that bold adolescent who responded to criticism with ease. I was just the opposite. I learned how to suck it all up, never forget about it, hold it in, and then blow up. For twenty-nine years, I thought this was normal. I did not think ill of it, and I sure did not question if it could bear that much weight. I just did it.

And then my emotions festered.

Friends came, and friends left. I was hurt, and I hurt them too. We were toxic. Relationships came and dragged itself, went over the moon, dipped inside the deepest waters, scrolled through a park, the whole nine yards, before breaking and leaving an even bigger hole in my tampered heart. I was hurt, and I hurt them too. Patterns in my relationships followed a particular style.

- I can fix them. I mean, no one is perfect; I just need to do the right things and say the right words. I can make this work.
- He is not working now, and he has not been keeping jobs, but I will help him. I will show him that I will not leave him, especially now.
- He is so hurt. Those girls broke him. He is safe with me. I will never allow him to hurt with me. I will protect his heart.
- He is so put together. Wow, I do not even have to fix him, but he is so stingy with money and his emotions. Well, I will say the right words and show him that I am not like those girls he invested money and time on while they were robbing him. I will show him I am different.
- Gosh, I am not attracted to him. I find him gross. But no one is perfect. I have seen people make this work, and I do not want to push him away, and then I am to blame. Let me close my eyes and make it work.

Yes, I was that toxic, not just in relationships by attracting toxic friendship and men, but I was toxic even in my own thoughts. I believed that because my father and I did not have any relationship, something was wrong with me. I believed that just because I could not connect with those around me, I was weird. I believed that just because I loved "me time"and I loved my own company, that when people judged me by saying I was eccentric, that they were right, and I was really weird. I believed that just because I desired marriage before having children, when I did not see that being practiced around me, that I was not normal. Are you seeing how my mind took the best of my personality, my values, etc. and turned them into negatives just because I began believing what people believed about me?

Through enduring years of pain and not having a decent outlet, I learned to allow it to fester until I realized that I, too, have the potential to be emotionally abusive. By sharing a dorm room with roommates who planned not to speak with me, whether in or out of the room, and not responding to my "good mornings." I was further pushed to the side in rejection. I could only lick my wounds. I turned on myself and that huge critical voice, usually in the tone of the first abuser, started playing again: "I'm not good enough." "I did something wrong, again." "What could I have done wrong to cause my friends, two friends who lived with me on dorm, to just get up one day and stop talking to me, but talk to each other?" "Why does the conversation in the room go around me?" "What the hell did I do wrong?"

These thoughts, in my mind, of course, were toxic, but in that moment, I could not shake the feeling that I must have blundered, terribly. I just could not put my finger on a specific thing. What I could have done, instead, is to learn how to adapt to the change and by so doing, sit with myself. I could have chosen to understand that people change, often. The only person I can change is me. What I could have done in that moment was to choose how I was going to respond to them.

31

Finally, I asked both of them why neither of them spoke to me anymore and why the conversations "go around" in the room without my inclusion. The answer I was given seemed like a slap. I mean, I blinked twice: "You are always out in the lounge, as if we are hurting you inside the room. You are not innocent in this. People see you in the lounge and are starting to wonder if we are doing something to you."

I did not figure this out until now. Right as she said this, I interpreted this to mean that to please them, I had to limit the time I spent doing my course pieces inside the lounge, while being mindful that people are watching in case I overstay in the lounge area. At that time, I felt disgusted by her response.

Now, looking back at the entire scenario, I understand where she may have seen this as hurtful. She had a rather questionable lifestyle, and some persons knew about it, so they could have been wondering if I found out, so I decided to stay my distance. Now, if I had known what she was into, I would have left the room; I ended up leaving shortly after, but I would have left earlier.

In no way, shape or form was their reason justifiable. It was wrong. It was not healthy. At least, a discussion would have sufficed first, from either party, before planning to stop speaking with me. However, I understand now that she had been hurt and had not dealt with her internal wounds. When she realized I enjoyed time by myself and in the lounge, she interpreted, based on her hurt, that I was rejecting her. It had nothing to do with the room or me.

The popular quote, "Hurt people hurt people," at that time, was alien to me. I learned of this after college. It justified, as it is meant to, the actions of those who hurt me without deliberately irritating them. It answered the question that because they too were hurt, it gave them a non-judgmental reason or unbiased understanding that they too were

32

most likely to hurt others. In most cases, hurt people rarely hurt their abusers; they end up hurting innocent people.

However, when I notice that I, too, became a victim of "hurt people" and I also had those inner wounds that would not heal because I did not even know what healing was, like I said earlier, I was just walking around, choosing people through the lens of my wounds and attracting more hurt people to cause further damage. At that turning point, I wanted to give myself that same unbiased understanding that because I was hurt, it was okay for me to now unleash on another innocent person, but something nudged me softly—something above my chest region. I began asking myself, "Do hurt people really have to hurt people?" I began delving deep inside my cave of bottled emotions.

I learned, in that moment, how to sit with myself and get to know myself before I was hurt.

I realized that I was such a bold person. Some may have called me a no-nonsense type. I also realized that I loved when people were happy, and when I was happy and full of life. I realized that I wanted peace and that I loved peace. I realized that I valued my freedom and that I loved myself to bits. I have truly grown not to mumble, "I love myself," to try to convince myself (passed this stage; it is a process), but now I truly do love my own self to bits and pieces. I realized that my voice is huge. I mean, before getting to know myself, I was stuck on what people thought about me. I was stuck on how they labeled my colour (Coppa cola/Coppa coloured is a derogatory term meaning dirty coloured). I was stuck on how they labeled my nose, "wide/big."

I was stuck on how they compared me to those who were worthless, "wuckliss." So, I began believing them. The moment I decided to sift through the mud and ugly mire of bullying, hatred, gossiping, abuse, ridicule, rejection, etc., and found myself, I realized how lovable, smart, lively, crazy talented, warm, promising, and damn beautiful I

33

am and will continue to be. I found my own heart, and though stabbed, left for dead, poisoned with hatred and ridiculed, rejected and smeared with blood, my heart beats just as powerfully. Even when the "thuds" are faintly recorded, my heart had vigor, and it just would not die.

Healing, my friends, is not for those who caused you pain. Accept now that some abusers, some manipulators, and some narcissists (especially the narcissists) will never change. Your duty is to love your own self and create healthy boundaries in your own life. If you are able, love some from a distance and keep it moving. Life is too enjoyable to be pushing a grown adult up a mountain. Stop pushing him/her to love you. Stop pushing him/her to marry you. Stop pushing him/her to tell you, "I forgive you." Stop training a grown adult. You are not God. Let God be God. You and I are flesh, blood and spirit. God is Spirit. If they will not allow the light of God to shine on their own hearts and lives, if they do not want to turn a new leaf, if they do not want to be disciplined enough to hear another perspective other than their own, can you outdo the Higher Authority who blew breath into them?

Listen, I have often heard this, and now I believe: "God is a gentleman/gentlewoman." Meaning, God will not force someone to do anything. So why do we kill ourselves for people? Do good to them, yes. Do good. Be respectful (especially if those who abused you are your parents). If you can, pray for them. In the same light, be good to yourself and those who are good to you. Be respectful to your own body, mind, and spirit. Do not harm yourself, and pray daily for yourself as well. You cannot give someone something that you do not possess.

Can Therapy Help?

As a Jamaican and, by extension, individual with a Caribbean background, I have never seen an individual or couple who has gone for therapy. I am assuming this is because of my environment. Maybe if I lived in another environment in Jamaica or in the diaspora, I would say differently. But, I have never read on social media pages about a fellow Jamaican going for therapy. Some of us as Caribbean people are taught that "God can fix it" while some are taught to forget the abuse/misfortunes/pain, suck it up, and "tough it out"(meaning grow stronger than the hurt). May I submit to you that emotional trauma and wounds fester just the same and, in some cases, worst than they do in the physical body. Do you not know that in order for your physical body to experience an illness, it was already lingering in your mind and emotions? If you are not sure about what I claim, you can research what scientists have discovered about the subconscious mind. Dr. Bruce Lipton (I am not affiliated with him, nor am I advertising for him) has done extensive work in this area. His work has opened my eyes, and practicing repetition has healed me tremendously.

An Analogy

To make it simpler for you, the subconscious mind is the part of ice-berg that you do not see. It is beneath the water. The conscious mind is the ice that you see.

The subconscious mind controls habits that we give no thought to: brush your teeth, yawning, laughing, white lies, blushing, walking, speaking, practicing a new language, then becoming fluent in it, blinking, etc. The conscious mind controls in the moment decisions: deciding on a trip to Jamaica, choosing a red jacket over a blue one, choosing tea over coffee, discussing a topic with your colleagues, etc. So, the subconscious is the autopilot while the conscious is the active pilot, making active decisions in that moment. Regardless of how sweet or cheerful/nice/warm the active pilot is (maybe six hours of the day), the autopilot (the remaining eighteen hours) will take over. The true person behind the active pilot will now take control.

That is similar to Dr. Jekyll and Mr. Hyde. It is very important, then, to know yourself. Reading this book may help you for one hour. What you can remember from this book at the end of three/six months is what was placed on autopilot. Autopilot is not a one, two or three times thing. It takes years of practice and repetition. There is no fast way to heal; notice how this chapter is extensive? There is no one way either. I am simply sharing my discoveries and what worked for me. In order to find out if you are wounded, you will have to pay keen attention to your autopilot. You do not have to like what you see or hear, but pay attention to it. It may save your life.

Healing The Mind

I have no training in medical practices, nor am I certified, but I have made this observation. In Jamaica, some of us like to label individuals with emotional wounds as "mad." The term is derogatory, and I think it gives those pointing the fingers a false sense of superiority. When calling someone "mad," these same persons doing so have no idea that whatever they release in the universe bounces back on those who released it. We need to be careful how we treat those among us with severe emotional wounds, and it seems like they have lost hope or the fight with it. Let us be mindful that emotional wounds fester, and it can fester anywhere, at any time, in anyone, and even if you did something fifty years ago, even at your ripe old age, that emotional wound may just fester.

Chapter Four: Healing Brew Part 2

Abused and Abuser: Help For Those In Need

Depression is a real thing. There is nothing weird about being deeply sad and hurt. When a person is depressed, he/she prefers to shut within themselves. That is fine. They should be encouraged to do so along with counseling, eating food high in antioxidants, etc. They can set reminders too, that what they are encountering is their emotional wounds on autopilot. One cannot defeat in a day, a twenty, forty, sixty years worth of repetition of emotional wounds that have now festered. What they can do or have someone do for them, is to play a recording (put it in their ears) of positive words, affirmations, playfulness, etc. It would even be better if the individual recorded in their own voice and play it back to themselves every night until self-hate/self-doubt/fear is replaced with its opposite. This is very important.

Those who have seemingly lost the battle with their emotional wounds/pain and are now harming themselves should never be left alone. They should be cared for, even to a greater extent, and more grace should be handed to them. Remember, no one was born "mad," and I cannot stop using "mad" in this way because I want Jamaicans to understand how truly weird this word is to be describing such a delicate matter. No one was born with a festered, open emotional wound. It was placed there in childhood. This is the sole reason why therapy is key. Therapists and trained psychiatrists know that in order to understand the adult language of you and me, they need to understand our childhood language. You may have seen in the previous chapters that I included a section called "Dear Inner Child," and this was deliberate.

In order to find out who adults are, dig into their childhoods. Let me go back on point. During childhood, it is no rocket science that children are like sponges; they soak everything up, and where does it go? Yup. Their subconscious mind. Every child came into this world already programmed to love. Children unconditionally love their parents, regardless of, in spite of. That is why an eight-year-old child who was raped by her own father, and having seen him with women, is led to jealousy and begins to find ways to seduce him back into having sex with her. It is wrong, but the child, the baby, unconditionally, loves her father. That is why a five-year-old child will do just about anything to stop her mother from screaming at them and will believe the lies her mother tells her and not see anything wrong with it and later on in life adapts to become a people-pleaser. It is wrong, but the baby, unconditionally, loves her mother. That is the autopilot.

Billions of adults, including myself, have been stuck or are still stuck with a childhood that may have had everything except love. They were rejected, teased about their weight/body, bullied because of their eyes/ears, etc., medical problems, experienced favouritism within their family, were made to feel ashamed because they had reading disabilities, and the list is endless. Many children soaked up those lies and have grown into shells of adults while their inner child wears all the emotional trauma and wounds. This is where the adult's autopilot rests.

Daddy's little girl, but daddy, where are you?

Case Study

Tasha lives with her mother and grandmother. She knows who her father is, and her mother doesn't make it difficult for him to come see her. In fact, she would encourage him to see her (Tasha), even if he doesn't have any lunch money, just to talk and show her that he is there for her. But there is always an issue that he has to deal with so he doesn't show.

Tasha goes to see him. They did not talk much because he was busy. Still immersed in work, he promised to buy her a gift for her upcoming birthday so she should go back home. She did. Overjoyed that her father made her a promise and that he actually cares, she reminded him what he promised, especially as her birthday draws near. With him, it was always, "I'll buy it tomorrow." Finally, her birthday came, and she was confident that her daddy would get it, because he remembered that today was her birthday. Face to face, as she asked him for her gift, he shouted at her, "Whey u a badda badda mi fah gal?" Translation: "Why the hell are you disturbing me, little girl?" Tasha felt something twist in her gut, way down below. She felt sick, like she received a blow that gave her a sinking, dizzy-like feeling. All at once, she knew she had done something wrong, again. She also confirmed that she could not do anything right, and she blamed herself for disturbing her father. Most of all, she wanted to make things right with him so that he did not stay mad at her.

There are thousands of "Tashas" in the black community. I speak from the standpoint of a young Jamaican lady having lived in Jamaica all my life. This is what I observed daily and is similar to the stories of young ladies I have mentored. "Tasha" will grow up into womanhood. She may struggle to get herself a degree, a beautiful house, or car. She is intelligent, friendly, warm-hearted, and full of life. She seems happy and fulfilled, but the romantic relationships of most of these ladies are "black love struggles." The subconscious mind recorded all that she felt about her father and all that she believed about herself.

As little girls who had abusive/absentee/narcissistic fathers, on a subconscious level, the message is, "I did something wrong to upset daddy; I will not do it again. I must be good." With this tiny seed or recording being played all the way into their adult lives, these young ladies seem to be established externally, but internally, it is the total opposite. Apart from low self-esteem, they may believe that they have little to no self-worth; they may also believe that they have to "work" for a man's love and that they must do all within their power to keep that man. In conflict, they may hold the belief that, indeed, they are correct in a given argument, but their minds will find one "good" thing about the man, and they may feel like they are betraying the man if/when they walk away. In other words, the wounds that "Tasha" had, have not healed at all. Like open sores, the old wounds have festered. It may be difficult for these ladies to let go of an abusive partner, regardless of the suffering she is enduring. If the man leaves her, she may feel as if her whole essence has left with him.

Of course, this could go another way. "Tasha" could have been guided to acknowledge what her internal triggers were, then worked them out and gone on to live her best life to the extreme. She may even marry a man who treats her with respect, one who provides and protects her at all costs while enhancing her happiness. It could happen. In fact, it does happen, but it does not happen enough in the black community. Ladies like "Tasha" seldomly have older women to guide them through and help them to navigate their triggers by digging deep within their internal beliefs. Most older women that I have encountered are "Tashas" themselves, and they have no idea. In this case, ignorance, for them, is bliss, and while it hurts to see beautiful, intelligent young ladies give away their immortality in exchange for all types of abuse, I now understand why they do. The black community, with regards to most black matriarchs, have shamed women who are of a certain age with no children or "man" to show. Regardless of some women's successful achievements, they may never be acknowledged as successful except their wombs work or they get married. Even further than that, a young lady, especially those who have spent time with themselves, who are thought of as successful, may not be hasty in settling down because she now identifies her triggers and wish not to repeat the toxic cycle—she may be labeled among her friends, relatives, matriarchs and even colleagues. It is true that misery loves company, but so does happiness and bliss; until black women from all regions, realize that we were lied to about our worth, dignity, womb, and place within the society, misery will win.

Black women, we were robbed by our parents, grandparents, uncles, stepfathers, stepmothers, brothers, and the list goes on. It can be argued that they did not know any better, and in truth, many did not have anyone to teach this to them. They just went about having relationships, and many women ended up with children on their own. But now we are living in a new era. I want to pass this baton to you, your girls, and those to come. The greatest relationship is not with our fathers, etc. who have harmed us; it is not with those who choose to love us either; it is with ourselves.

41

Your greatest relationship is the one you have with you.

Have a great friendship and lasting relationship with yourself. This is true magic.

Abusive Relationships

For those of you living in abusive relationships, it is easier said than done, but please leave. Plan, be proactive. Save some money. If there is someone you can trust, please borrow.

Speak to a counselor. Based on your location, find hotlines that respond quickly to domestic violence.

Wait until he/she is gone.

Do not take any furniture. Sometimes, all you need is you, your child, and your lives and the clothes on your back. God will provide. Run with your life.

Do not tell anyone that is close to him/her.

Relocate. Go somewhere that no one knows you.

Develop a skill or apply for a job. Maybe some of you are asking why relocate without a job, and this is serious. However, only an abused individual knows the hell he/she is living in. Let nothing come before your life. Ensure that you take your certificates/degrees/birth papers, ID, Passport, etc., so that applying for a job or starting a small business (if it is even to sell on eBay) will be easy.

If necessary, change your name quickly.

Reach out to a church that has programs to help you heal.

It is never too late to start over.

Open Your Eyes

If a person, whether in jokes, between laughs, or in a serious tone, tells you that he/she will slap you, believe them. Do not stay to find out how hard that slap will be.

If someone tells you he/she will kill you, believe them. Do not stay. The world needs you to be alive. Do not let a man or a woman dominate themselves over you. Do not allow your life to be cut short in the name of domestic violence.

If someone is in the same space as you but barely talks to you, blames you for little mistakes, wants you to be their slaves, do not become a modern-day Cinderella, do not allow anyone to bleed on you if they do not want to heal. You cannot deplete your energy rescuing another. Who told you that after they are in a better place in life, with your help, that they will return the favour? Recommend counseling for them, share with them how you can, but, my friend, your safety, and peace of mind must come first.

If your friends gossip about you, maybe one came to you and told you what the other says, I would advise you to choose better friends. You deserve it.

If you are a woman and you have children with multiple partners with/without a steady partner in the home, I would advise you to seek counseling and wisdom. Avoid speaking highly of one child while putting another down. Avoid retelling nasty jokes or stories about a child's father, especially while discussing with another child or your partner. It will deplete your children's confidence, and arrogance will breed in your home. Sibling rivalry will have just begun, and you will wonder, in your old age, why your children are all scattered. Get counseling for yourself, forgive yourself, and heal so you do not end up bleeding on your children.

If you are a married woman who has just suffered an affair, do not, I repeat, do not bleed on your children/child. Get a counselor if you cannot cope. If you can, journal. Find help in therapy and let professionals help you to heal. Get healing for yourself so that your confidence is renewed and you decide whether you will leave or stay—either way, set healthy boundaries. Do not take out your anger on the children/child and do not replay the horrendous act to your child, whether male or female.

If you are a man who has not fathered your children and if you are serious about wanting a relationship with them, or if you are not sure, my friend, close the book. Come back when your mind is mind up.

(For fathers who are serious) If you are not living with them, contact the mother, and show her that you would like to have a relationship with them. Meet with them in public with the mother. Express your fears as a younger version of yourself and take your share of the blame. Build trust with them. If you live with them, but you are emotionally detached or unavailable, go get counseling. Only invite them in when your mind's made up to be consistent in showing them your love. Do not pull them in and push them away.

If you were a member of a church or spiritual/religious organization that did you wrong and now you are questioning every single thing you were taught while associating with them, you are not the first, my dear, and you will not be the last. It is unfortunate. I am sorry that you experienced this type of hurt. It shows that no one can be fully trusted, except God. Regardless of the title of a man, the man is a man first. Regardless of the title of the woman, she is a woman first. Give yourself grace. You trusted the wrong people, so have I and so many others. Give yourself time. Do not hold on to grudge. It will seem nice to do, but it is a setup. Listen, those persons may have hurt you and did you wrong, and they may very well go and ask God quietly to forgive them, and it is done. Now, are they off the hook? Oh no; whatever a man sows, that he will reap, but the difference is, God's love is unbiased. It will see them through. If you hold on to the pain and grudge, it will now fester, and you will forget the good they did. No one person is 100% evil. There has to be even 1% good that they taught you. Hold on to that and, slowly but surely, forgive them. I am not suggesting you knock down their doors, calling their phones yelling, "I forgive you!" but forgive them quietly and set healthy boundaries. You teach someone how to treat you.

Quietly go before your Papa and ask Him to help you release this hurt, especially if it is religion-related. When our own parents fail us (because their parents failed them) and friends failed us, relationships are abusive as hell, and we are strung out on drugs, nearly killing ourselves, our last resort is usually religion. Now, when spiritual leaders fail us, it is as if God himself rejected us. That is how we interpret it, and we wonder if God is indeed love or real. Remember, religious institutions are indeed hospitals. Some patients are responding to treatment, some do not want it, even to save their lives, some are healed, but mentally, they want to be sick because they like the free food and attention from friends and family. While you cast this care on Papa, give yourself some grace. Those same people are hurting too. Do not let their salary or their perfect family or smiling faces fool you. There is something lurking somewhere that sometimes, even their own husbands or wives or children know nothing about.

If you are an abusive parent, get counseling as soon as possible. Do not delay. Take responsibility for your dilemma. Abusing your children may give you a certain "kick" or "high" because they are vulnerable and trusting, but I guarantee you that they will grow up one day. The one(s) you hurt the most, will in turn, hurt you when you least expect it, also when you are most vulnerable. The one(s) who you valued as the "golden child/children" may grow into a greater monster than you were/are and, in your old age, may also bully and belittle you. Stop bleeding on your children if you are going through it. They are not adults. Show them how to be a healthy, responsible adult who will now foster a mutually healthy relationship with a partner, thereby raising decent people. God has blessed you with children; they remain the heritage of God. Abusing them is making a mockery of God. If they become a handful, ask for wisdom to know how to approach them. If they are toxic or demean you, set proper boundaries in place and then get help for them. At no time should you allow them to disrespect you. God has used you to usher them in on this Earth. At no time should you choose to abuse them, whether deliberately or on autopilot. Choose better.

If you are a child porn dealer/enabler or viewer, it is not well with you. If you do not see your act as an evil thing, if you do not see your own mess, it will never be well with you if you do not see how imbalanced you are. Your eyes will not know light. Your mind will have no safe place to rest. May you succumb to your harvest of that which you have sown until you choose better for yourself. May the blood, tears, and sweat of those children be upon your head and follow you through the generations. I will not have mercy, and I will not mince my words on this one. As a people, we should call a damn spade a spade. The poorest to the richest class indulge in child pornography, regardless of whatever role they play. It. Is.Wrong. It is not well with you. May the fire of the wisdom of God lead you to your demise if you do not get help. Sir, you are sick. Find a hospital, counseling, therapy. Madam, you are sick. Find counseling and therapy. Some of you reading this are apart of this circle. You have already decided what you will do. If you stay on that path of destruction, God is still God, and it will rain, and the sun will shine either way. Help will come for the multitude of

46

children that you have hurt, whose blood the Earth is drunk with. Help will rise from somewhere for them. But for you and yours, ah!

Our world is broken because our families became broken and since we have folded our arms and refused to heal ourselves, while at the same time, we are all pointing on each other because this and that and this one caused us hurt, and we start obsessing with, "God will chastise them/karma will get them/God will prepare a table in the presence of my enemies."

I can imagine God saying, "Well, children, you are all Mine. Show one another love, be kind to your neighbour, show respect to your elders, love yourselves, love Me because I am love," yet no one wants to make the first move, so we continue quarreling and fighting. We fight in our families; we fight across countries, we fight for oil, we fight, we fight, we fight; we blame the younger generation by saying, "You know back in my days, we had respect! If we did what you youths today are doing...." Well, maybe if the youths today had normal, healthy childhoods in each family, those same youths would grow into interdependent, nurturing, responsible, and sharing adults and would choose similar partners and produce even healthier babies. I hope this is what the "new world" brings. This adult is tired of all this fighting.

Message To My Inner Child

My hands are yours to hold. Here's my shoulders, baby, come and rest. Release the years of bickering, strife, and defeat. Release. Release. Release. You are now safe. I apologize for those who caused you harm. You were abused, and it was wrong. Unfair. Unjust. You may be wondering now, where do we go from here? Let me hold your hand. Hand in hand, together we are strong. I don't have all the answers, and I can't promise you that you will never hurt again, but I'm going to

47

hold on to your hand as we walk, dance, skip on our journey, reaping beauty from the ashes thrown our way.

Signed _____   Date _____

Poem: Yes, I Trust You

No food in my pot
But I trust You with my whole life
No marriage proposal yet
But I trust You with my whole life
Ha! I'm yet to pay off my debt
Still, I trust You with my whole life
Our babies are hungry
I trus --- wait ---
Can't You see the children cry?
Is it fair?
Tell me, is it?
To trust a God unseen for things that we all see
And touch
And taste
Can't You see the little boy raped?
Can't You see that man in the corner,
Tired with shame?
What about me?
And me?
And me?
How do You say, "My dear, I love you."
Should I really, still trust You?
Do You really understand pain?
Can You bear an unbearable burden?
Can You race me to my troubles that seem so dare?

Why? Are You near?
Or are You so distant
That I can hardly hear You mumbling, "Peace, My dear."
So,
I am tired of trusting
Tired now of faith
Tired of church hurt and abuse
Of being used
Of being accused
Of being a tool
Of being hated and ridiculed
Who is the one to fight my battles?
Why do You step in right before my death?
Where is my peace?
Or am I suffering my ancestors' curses?
Where is *my* peace?
I want to argue with You
I want to tell You, "It isn't alright."
I want to cry against You
I just want to feel Your devotion and love for me
Just
This
Once
So, where are You?
Trusting You?
That's too big
Too big for narc survivors
Too big for abused people healing
Too big for mother and fatherless children
Too big for me

Why don't we start over?
I'll drop tradition

I'll drop how I was taught to pray
I'll drop titles and long eloquent speeches
I'll drop speaking with tongues
Because I don't always want to, anyways
I'll drop my mask of religion
I'll drop my mask of atheism
I'll drop my mask of, well, me
Are You ready?
Let me see You
No, wait,
Let me know you in the fullness of Your resurrection power
Simply put, let's have our own relationship!
No one else
Just us
Let's take it back at one
I am Your child
You are Father
I am Your child
You are Mother
Show me that You love me
Unconditionally
Talk to me with kindness
Feed my spirit
Tell me I'm beautiful and adored
I am gentle, so be gentle with me
Show me the little things
And the big ones
Hold my hands tightly
Hug me slowly
Never ever let go

I don't want Your religion
I don't want Your checklist

Poem: Yes, I Trust You

I just want You.
While we develop a relationship
Healthy relationship
It is in this that I will
I shall
Yes, I trust You.

Chapter Five: Thanksgiving Brew

On Matters of Thanksgiving

*M*y previous relationship was what I thought was golden. He and I seemed perfect together. He had even ticked some of my written Godly husband characteristics. All seemed forward-moving, and then we became engaged. But we had no peace. That coupled with his derogatory "slip" of the tongue were only in private, but when I reacted, it became a public show. He was certainly not a villain, and I, not an angel; we were incompatible and toxic for each other. But I wrestled with this as I did not want to end it because knowingly if I called it off, I knew fingers would point at me, even if behind my back.: "I am the problem," so I started thinking: "Should I take what I got and shut up? Am I kidding myself to believe that I deserve a Godly man who protects, provides, respects, and loves me? Is this my best?"

I struggled internally while plastering a smile on my face. I just could not take it anymore, so I prayed. It was a heartfelt prayer. This time, I did not pray about him and I as a team. In His sovereignty, I asked God to show me this man's heart, so I could have peace in marrying him. Three weeks later, he made another degrading "slip" of the tongue, and I ensured that this was the last slip. I boldly returned his ring and called it quits. I mustered all the courage and might within me to believe that if he was like this now, he will be ten times as worse after marriage, and looking back on that day, weak as I was, I knew deep down that I deserved better. His pleas were ignored and, friends, I can tell you that it was God who firmly held me in that period; as I said before, he was not a villain, and I could overlook verbal abuse as I had seen other women do, but I decided to choose better for myself. Best. Decision. Ever.

The aftermath was not easy. I went through many ideas to cope: Would I now "link" back an ex? Could I be what boys are by being the "friend with benefits" type? Do I even want to entertain another man?

Finally, it had to take the grace of God to steer those thoughts away from my mind and instead plunged me into deep waters of finding my own worth, on my own, not in a man or in material things. What a journey that was. It started off bitter, really bitter, but what a glory has now risen on me. I can firmly say that I can feel my Papa's light shining warmly on me.

I have looked back on strings and strings of bad habits, wrong choices in men, broken relationships, a relationship that I thought I had manifested with God's help, friends who I thought were the cats' "Meow" and the list goes on and on; I now surely thank God a little louder than I did years prior.

My love language with God runs on the basis of: Words of Affirmations and Acts of Service; you heard me right. God and I have a love language.

My morning routine is opening my eyes and saying something like "Papa, thank You. Thank You for keeping me since last night. Thank You that I wasn't afraid. Thank You that my mind went to rest," then I reach for my gratitude list (4 pages) and with squinted eyes, read through word for word, feeling and tasting the words while acknowledging that what I am grateful for has truly come to pass.

Being grateful has saved my life in three ways:

1. My mind is at peace, so I can think more clearly.
2. I had trust issues with God! I now TRUST that God is my Papa and He is only working for my good.
3. I keep a record of all the good things and great gifts Papa sent my way. Even the not-so-good people or gifts, I have learned to sift through and find a 1% of good in them and use it to my advantage.

I now thank God for closing relationship doors, some I banged on for years and years on end. Some, I sat down at the closed door, believing and hoping that God will open the door for me with time. Some, I thought I would "convince" God that I was worthy of the man so I would "work" for God so He would reward me. During those moments, now reflecting, God was just silent while holding my hands through it all. The only time I "heard" the voice of the Holy Spirit was when I was between a rock and a hard place in terms of relationships. Here is how the story went.

Story Time

In 2015, I started my first job. I had met a great guy who pursued me relentlessly, and I knew this was a good thing solely because the YouTube couple videos I had watched spoke about a Godly man pursues a woman he is interested in. So here was this guy, great and all and pursuing me. I knew to ease away and seek the face of God for clarity. I did just that. During that week, I went to a fasting service, and a week prior, I had made it known that I was taking a break to get myself together. I did not reveal to the person that I was going to pray and seek God. After returning home, I dropped to my knees and prayed. I simply asked God what role this man played in my life. I knew something was off, and I sensed that I wanted this to be "it" so badly because I was not used to this level of pursuit. Honestly, I was not. I kept hearing in my heart, "No, no, no." Anyway, I climbed into bed, dismissed what I heard, and started listening to "Fly" by Jason Upton and an Angel. About twenty minutes in, I heard a clear, calm, authoritative voice speaking clearly to me. I was not afraid, nor did I look around, but I knew this was as close as God would get to me to hear Him like this. The Holy Spirit said clearly: "What do you want? Do you want to live the life you've always wanted to have: the boys, parties, dating, etc.? Do you want to marry who you want to marry, travel when you want to travel, etc.? Or will you listen to Me, submit, and trust that I have your heart's desires for you? Reflect carefully and tell me what you decide. Whatever you ask, I will do."

I took a deep breath. I knew this was the precious Holy Spirit. After about one hour and a half, I spoke back, audibly as well: "God, I cannot lie to You. You already know what I want. I want the life with the boys, traveling, etc., but what I NEED is to know You in the fullness of Your resurrection power."

At this point, the Holy Spirit began revealing some information about future events and had not said, even to this day, anything about the decision I had made. I only saw my life unfolding based on what I had decided.

The same person the Holy Spirit told me to avoid was who I chose to be with. It took some time, but God is wise, and so He gave the individual an opportunity that he simply could not resist. There goes our relationship with the opportunity.

I went through broken relationships one after the other. Another phase of broken "situationships" all because I got "real and raw" with God. I went through periods of relocating to two countries for work without asking Papa, and just like that, all my year's savings blew up like dry bamboo wood. For two years, I hit rock bottom on matters of love/relationships and finances. Two solid years and it was not consecutive, so I would build up myself and then invest in a job opportunity for the second time in a totally different country and job type, but the result was the same. I returned home with 75% of my savings gone. Vanished.

So, I picked up my broken pieces the third time around, and in May of 2020, I began fasting, and while doing this fast, I started giving God thanks. I had a lot to complain about: a house I had applied for was rescheduled to be completed later in the year; giant doubts formed in my mind about my worth, my past came up literally; someone from my past thought it cute to want to "be friends" with me and I just had to make it known for the billionth time that that door was sealed shut. I walked away from "friends," and I had no mentor.

So, though my troubles seemed small, it was a major deal for me since I was being hurt exactly where my old wounds were.

I began finding recent to older things that God had made right in my life and, man, were there some major ones. The COVID-19 situation came up when I needed a mental break from my job to just rest and get back in touch with myself. So, on March 12, in the night, I broke down in tears for hours, and I mean hours. Snot, tears, mouth drool, everything was on display while I knelt down at the foot of my bed tearing silently. The tears that were buried for every single pain I had endured came to the surface and washed over that night. When I was finished, I felt light. I felt like a feather among feathers. To top it off, I told Papa that I was so stressed at work, but I appreciated that He provided it for me so I could save. With that, I slept.

The following day, in the last thirty minutes of the day before the dismissal bell, the Prime Minister had announced a closure of schools islandwide given the recent COVID-19 discovery hours before. Even while writing this and reliving the experience, I remembered how I cried for hours without making a sound since I learned to cry internally while tears spill externally. I also remembered my last request before sleeping and then to discover the following day that I was allowed to work from home for two weeks, Government orders! Of course, those weeks expanded into months, not without challenges, but still, gratitude prevails. So, back on point, I reminded God of how He did this for me; no one heard or knew about the other miraculous things He did just for me. The more I reminded God, I also reminded myself, and I began to lean in on God's love for me. I began to see that God listens to me. I began to understand that God is watching over me, not from an unseen place in the sky or in heaven, whether above or below, but that God is in here in my little room, on my bed, sitting right beside me and recording every request and counting and wiping every teardrop.

Every time I gave thanks for the simplest things: I can see, I can sit upright, my limbs are working, I am in my right mind, I am able to think and talk straight, etc., I am reminded that no matter what happens or will happen, that there is a greater, higher force that wants to see me win and will do anything possible to see me through to the end.

I began to remind God that He is my Father and Mother, and just like that, in the mornings, I "big up" God. I am a lover of seafood, so sometimes, I say:

- "Papa, You are my steamed fish and okra."
- "You are my coconut run-down with salt mackerel."
- "Papa, you are my escovitch fish and cheesy broccoli."
- "You are my coconut water, very chilled!"
- "You are my pure water (room temp)."
- "You are my green plantain, crushed and fried."

As you can imagine, as I speak that into the loving God-like force in my life, this same force/love that I call God sends even more back to me. In that time, I have learned that whatever I am grateful for and say "thank you" to actually multiplies. Thank you, Rev. Funke Felix Adejumo. I found her on Youtube. Please, watch her sermons.

Over this period, the latter part of my special request in 2015 to the Holy Spirit has also manifested: "I NEED to know You in the fullness of your resurrection power."

I cannot tell you where that came from in that moment, neither while reflecting on it now. I do not know. It just came out of my mouth. I think, though, it had something to do with wanting the truth about God because I was tired of the routine things in church. I was tired of having a long list of things God was upset with me about. I was tired of God seeming so cold and detached! So, I put in that request as well, which was the desire of my heart then. I knew that I had answered honestly about the life I wanted, and then I dropped in what I needed from God.

The Holy Spirit delivered each, on time.

Knowing what I know now, would I have asked differently? No, I would not because God already knows if I was pretending to be "good' or obedient just to get what He has on His heart for me. I did not want to play with something fictitious or something that had no depth. I wanted to know how deep God was, and, my friends, He called me on those waters!

Message To My Inner Child

Thank you for crying when you were sad. Thank you for laughing when you were happy. Thank you for showing me that my emotions matter. Thank you for being inquisitive about this place called Earth. Thank you for all that you went through; you made the decision to live, though you did not know how. But you are here, and because you lived, I live. My adult self looks polished with a family of my own, possessions, degrees, and even romantic interests. But you are at the pinnacle; you are my foundation; my Rock. Thank you.

Signed _____   Date _____

Poem: For All Those Times You Stood By Me

Papa, for all the ways You love me
Thank You
For being my strength when I was frail
Thank You
For seeing light within me when I was grime
I thank You
For being bones of my bones and flesh of my flesh
God within
Thank You
For wiping my tears and cheering me on towards the finish line
Thank You
For holding me in those warm nights,
Smoothing my cheeks and nestling me
Thank You
For holding me close away from the wolves and the sheep too
Thank You
For having called me Your own
Thank You
What in the world did I do to deserve this type of unselfish love?
Why in the world would You put your trust in me, a woman?
Why would You rely on me to get Your will done?
Why do You look at me and remember no more my sins?
Why do You call me "most blessed?"

Most loved of all women?
I can't say "Thank You" enough
I just want to be wherever You are
You are my truth
You are my light
You are my pleasure
You are my principle
You are my shine
Thank You
Thank You
Thank You
When mothers cradle their babies, so You cradle me
When mothers nurse their young ones, You do the same to me
When fathers instruct their child tenderly, so You look to me
When fathers gently kiss their daughters tears away,
From a broken heart, so You kiss my pain away
When the storm rages on
And the oceans foam and spit and fight
When my ship gets battered, torn, and old
And fish come up to share my bones
When the moon refuses to shine on me
No light for me to find my torch
When death sinks my ship
And cold piercing water reach in for the kill
I see the face of death glaring in my face
Red eyes to hazel green
With just a whisper, I mumble Your name
With my heart's final breath
I call You to rise
And with that, You search the heavens
Lift up the Earth
Scatter the stones
Desecrate the valleys

Uproot trees and mince kings and queens of wicked
You swoop down beneath the wretched deep
And there, with one look, evil shies away in fear
With just one glance, I am rescued
With strong open arms, you shoulder me
I am now lifted high, resurrected, I am on high
But when on the surface, I now see
I am astonished. How can this be?
Didn't You come from heaven to earth
Air to sea to rescue me?
I see a Earth untouched and order maintained
I look beneath the ocean's depth
And discover a world from which You came

Join Me

For

Tea

A Special Brew: 1 Tsp of Transparency, 9 Slices of Wisdom & 1 Tsp of Courage

Chapter Six: Transforming Brew

On Matters of Transformation

I am sure you have read or heard about the story, "The Ugly Duckling And The Beautiful Swan." I read the shortened version of this story when I was just twelve years old, just once, and it stuck in my memory; that and "The Princess and the Pea." Even at that age, I was "the odd one out," and it was no secret. Growing up as a teen, I seldom had long-lasting friendships and even relationships as an adult. When my peers would talk about slumber parties or meeting up at the library to study or just socializing on a Saturday evening at KFC, I thought *they were* weird. I wondered how they did it, and I wondered why. When I became an adult, I realized that forming healthy relationships was quite impossible. On a large scale, I read way more than any of the young men I dated. I asked much more critical questions about my existence, energy, the quantum world, life, and celestial things. When I did not have those questions, I spoke less, lesser than men "allegedly" spoke. I observed more, and I did the unfathomable: I started praying in my private time that God showed me who they really were.

As you can guess, God answered every single prayer, and looking back on those "situationships" now, they ended because I was "weird" enough to pray. I mean, who instructs their twenty-five-year-old to pray before entertaining a young man? Isn't he just a young man? But I learned the value of praying before entertaining a man, especially with regards to a serious relationship. Were my problems solved? Nope! After person A and I broke up, I placed myself to be found by person B, without giving myself time. So it went, one after the other.

At twenty-eight years old, I did not just have an exaggerated trail of splintered situationships and broken engagements; I also had a negative view of men. It just had to be them, right? I checked off the list in my mind of the plethora of "good" things that I contributed to those awkward hookups, yet they all ended, whether I wanted them to or not. I started praising myself even more because I saw myself as the golden woman, and, in my eyes, I was good. I just had not found the "right" man yet. And, I used the broken marriages and half relationships that I have observed in my environment to justify my subtle hostility towards men. After all, I saw some of them abusing their wives, consistently and constantly cheating on the "love" of their lives, and just treating them just about any way they subject them to. I did not want to walk in those women's shoes, so I told myself that I just had to wait and find the right man.

Then, there were those women who became tired of the abuse and neglect of their partners, so they too became abusers and master manipulators. The playing field could be leveled. I was at the crossroads without signposts. I was angry at God, angry at myself, and even more so at the men who did not protect my heart when I gave it to them. But I still desired a mate/life partner, so what could I do? I became even "weirder." I began asking God to step into my love life and friendships. I stopped dating. It just got hard, and I could not pretend to be interested when I was not. I will share why in a minute. Also, I completely removed friends/associates and past relationships, everything and anything that did not challenge me to be better. Anything that looked a lot like my triggers, anything that had a similar childhood to mine that refused to do the work and heal and anything that reminded me of a low time/space in my life, I released. Completely.

I began spending lots of time with myself. No one called my phone outside of family. No one messaged me outside of Whatsapp group messages from work. I began to listen. I began to feel. I began to get intimate with this girl, this woman called Roxanne Reid. Also, I began actively writing down my dreams. I saved my phone number and texted myself on Whatsapp. I know, weird! But I got that weird. I began encouraging myself through these text messages. I began reminding myself that the past hookups, failed engagement, etc. was not really me. I began telling myself that God must have had more in store for me. At this point, I had grown more in love with God and finally knew Him as the Spirit of Truth and Love. I held an image of God in my mind, which may shock you. This image was the beautiful face of a black woman, with soft angel eyes that saw and knew me, and a smile that communicated love and grace. She had the arms of a first-time mother, always outstretched, ready to hold me.

I held that image in my mind, and I started, truly, thinking about God as an expression of father and mother. I thought about the highest form of love I could receive from a father and mother and used this to recreate the knowledge of God. I no longer felt alone. I felt like I had parents beyond my wildest imagination who liberated me to love but who are always there when I needed their help, even when they do not agree.

I started to relax and really began enjoying my own company. I found myself researching quantum theories, moral compass debates, dimensions, and recently, the Biblical foundation of marriage. I also started zooming in to the Bible stories even more. It can be argued, maybe successfully, that the Bible accounts of whatever it reported are just stories. If that is true, then it is not a terrible thing because, after all, what isn't a story? Great lessons are created around a story, and characters bring to light hidden traits in all of us. My mind began to expand, and I began seeing my connection to God. No, I am not God (sorry New Agers), but I saw the divine essence of God within me. It is the vibration of my heart and yours. I also started seeing the good and bad in everything, including myself. I took the blame for the former petty relationships that I willingly chose to be a part of. I now know that since I was/am the only denominator in past relationships, I had to be the one doing something wrong.

Some of you may be wondering if I was that awful woman that put down the man or did not have anything to offer him—quite the opposite. Since there was no bond between my father and I (remember, the father is the first man who makes his daughter feels loved, protected, provided for, and cherished), and not having that, not having him in any meaningful way in my life, I believed a lie. I believed that once I encountered conflict, any kind, or any sign of danger, that I should take my leave. On the extreme opposite, I subconsciously attracted broken men, and I tried to fix them so they would know I was a "good" woman. Ultimately, I was doing too much to show my worth/value. I was busy doing too much. Once I learned this, that was the reason why I stepped back from dating and talking to men, period. But this was not the end because I learned how broken I was and that my childhood had a huge part to play in this.

None of us living under the sun has had a 100% flourishing childhood since we have all inherited some form of information/programming through the blood that runs through our veins. When I learned that Roxanne Reid is not just Roxanne Reid, per se, but that I carry information/codes from my mother and her family all the way into the generations, as well as my father and his family all the way into the generations, I was shell shocked. I knew then that every thought/habit/behaviour was not all mine, and I saw major patterns in my life that either reflected families of my mother's or father's lineage. I decided that I would not take the hurt or pain to my children or to anyone else for that matter. I decided that I was going to heal. I decided that I was going to transform into that beautiful Swan that I read once, just once, as a twelve-year-old.

Join Me

For

Tea

A Special Brew: 1 Tsp of Transparency, 9 Slices of Wisdom & 1 Tsp of Courage

Chapter Seven: Transforming Brew: Part 2

On Matters of Transformation

I began doing my inner work. Was it hard? You better believe it was not a joke. I have discussed the power of the subconscious mind, so retraining or rewriting codes for a child's subconscious mind is much easier than that of an adult. A child's subconscious mind has downloaded every single thing around him/her as much as to amplify information passed down through the bloodline by age seven. Imagine me, at age twenty-nine, discovering this? But I had a vision for my life. I did not know where I was going, and I still cannot be sure, but I know it is not swimming with the ducks. That would not work anyway because just like the swan, before it knew it really was a beautiful swan, everyone around this swan saw its ugliness; even Mother Duck in the story. She knew innately that this very ugly "duckling" was not hers. She must have kept her babies from it. Other animals and even people who saw it wanted to harm it. It always fell over something, tripped over something, scared someone away, and everywhere it went, people hid away from it. It was hideous, and as it grew, it became even more so.

It was on a warm summer day as it slept, it heard children's voices. They were filled with glee as they expressed their "ooohs" and "aaahs" at the myriads of beautiful, graceful swans. This "ugly duck, all grown" opened its eyes and prepared to run and hide itself because soon, it knew the children would see its face and would throw things, just like every other time. Imagine its surprise when, as soon as it rose up, the children exclaimed, "This is the most beautiful of them all!" and started petting and giving it food. The surprised "Ugly Duck" saw its reflection in a stream/lake, and it could not believe it. Staring back at him/her was a huge, graceful, gloriously white swan, perfect as a picture. It was right among its kind, and they all flew away. It was never ever lonely again. I am sure that there is something in this lesson for all of us; mine is: we become who we really are. Let that sink in.

But some of you may ask, "How do I know this if I do not know who I am?" Well, now that you asked, the answer is simple. Make a list of everything you are not. These can be things that do not sit well with you or things that you dislike. Start simple: list fifteen things that you are not. Write anything. Then, get another blank leaf and write fifteen things that you are. These can be things that you like (like attracts like). Now, make a list of the top five characters that you admire; characters from novels/stories and even in your life. We all play a character at times, but some of us may not know yet. Look at the characters that you admire and ask yourself:

1. Do I admire him/her for their kindness, or do I admire them because he/she is mean?

2. If I could get one wish, could I be like this character and still feel good about myself?
3. If this character was real, do I see myself hanging out with him/her?

I did an actual exercise of this, and I concluded that, let us call this character Mr. Dom with his grey shades. Though enigmatic and enthralling, I would happily skip over now. I no longer prefer impulsive behaviour or mercurial activity. I no longer prefer to feel love for someone who wants to hurt me to test his/her love for me (intimate and platonic relationships). Notice I said, I no longer prefer to feel love for! I said it correctly. Love, friends, is definitely a choice. I checked the other male romantic character of every girl's teenage love crush: the broad-chested, hot-tempered vampire, who fell in love after a thousand years. I realized that both characters, Mr. Dom and Mr. Drop Dead Gorgeous Vampire, are eerily similar. Both are mercurial, both repeated, "Stay away from me" to females they were interested in, both were controlling the monster within them, both had flaring tempers, both had "danger" written all over them—see my point? In addition to this, both significant others (girlfriends turn wives) are not off the hook though. Both are drawn to danger; both are saved by their partners, both are more courageous in love pursuits than their partners; both got married rather quickly and got pregnant which, at first, was difficult for their terrified partners. This was the essence of my personality as a teen and young adult. I woke up at twenty-nine and realized that I did not choose to be the saviour of male partners; I did not choose to go after the beast. It was a pattern passed down through the generations, and once I figured this out, I went back to the same stories to find other characters that I had missed. There had to be some in the background. There had to be even one who was calm, level headed, and most of all, emotionally opened.

Having done my inner work, I now prefer peace, humility, purpose and culture, so going back to the characters, I could confidently skip past Mr. Dom to the Hispanic artiste, and the level-headed fatherly vampire over Mr. Drop Dead Gorgeous any day of the week! Maybe I am "boring," and I like it.

After rediscovering who you are, it will be clearer to see and identify your kindred spirit in family, friends, and romantic pursuits.

Inner Work And Me

Some of you may be wondering what "inner work" means. This simply means knowing yourself for you, not what your genes make you. It is the conscious choice that you make to be yourself, whatever and whoever that looks like to you in your imagination. Most times, we experience brokenness, failed relationships, and friendships, among other things, because we carry unhealed emotional trauma inside.

Imagine a garbage truck that is broken down. It has scattered, literally, all the garbage right at your gate. You are in despair. You have invited some pretty powerful people to your home for Sunday brunch, so what now? Imagine yourself taking up some of the debris and sticking it inside your top until most of the garbage litter vanishes. Imagine yourself putting on an additional hoodie and zipping it right up, squaring your shoulders as your face forms a creaseless smile at the powerful people now approaching your house. Can you possibly imagine going around people with debris in your shirt, covered by a clean, warm hoodie? The thought is repulsive. Well, why are we so comfortable entertaining and putting on a show for others when the debris in our hearts need to be dealt with? Sooner or later, those people will smell the debris coming from the hoodie, and it will just be a matter of time before trails of garbage will now litter your house. Take this from me, hurt people carry debris. If you are hurt, choose to stop dating. Sort out your debris and empty them where they belong: in a trash can. Do not transfer the smell/fragrance of your hurt or the energy thereof to another. Hurt people do not always have to hurt people. Let us be this change so that finally, we can be transformed.

Transformation is change. It is the only thing in life that is constant. Embrace change. Do not let it play hide and seek with you. Stop running away from it. Confront change, especially yours, and step to it with love.

This is how I confronted changes in my life:

1. I cried, a lot. I then washed my face and moved forward.
2. I showed up afraid.
3. I stopped blaming people for my problems. Instead, I take responsibility for every good or evil in my life.
4. I began liking myself just the way I am in the moment that I am.
5. I spoke positively to change as if it were a person.
6. I sought my peace in the change.
7. If the change was consuming me, I pray for wisdom.
8. I imagine that each change is the next level to a good game.
9. I imagine that each change is a plot development in my life movie.
10. If the change is still not a blessing, I know it is not the final change.
11. I ask the change what lesson(s) it has for me to grow.
12. Before I step into another level of change, I take stock of what I learnt previously.

Message To My Inner Child

Hello baby, I bet you did not know, or would never guess that your life would have been this difficult. I bet you never dreamed up half of what has happened thus far. I guess now you are afraid of the future, afraid of what is to come. You can bet that whatever, and I mean, whatever happens, I will be right there. I am always right there. If you experience suffering to sheer happiness and joy, I will still be there. You are not alone on this path. So many other little ugly "ducklings" are out there, fighting their way through the grim and mud. Some are black, white, Asian, Mexican, Spanish, etc. Though they sound different, I promise you that they will find you. Your kind will find you.

Your grand spring of transformation is right now. Yes, this very moment. Let that sink in. You now realize who you are and why you are the way you are. Baby, you were never born to fit into any crowd. The crowd does not have what you do, and the crowd cannot give you what you have. You are the beautiful, graceful swan that is now seeing the other half of the truth. Your time of transformation has come, little one. Look and see! Your kindred spirits are all around, and they are beckoning you to fly; fly in a way you never have before. You have overcome. You did it. No one else could. You kept the faith. You lost many, many battles, baby, but you won the war.

Many things were used against you—your gender, nose, hair, skin colour, height, nationality—you now know how unique you are. You didn't know when, how, why, or what you did that made the world hated you so much. Guess what? You look like nothing, absolutely nothing you have been through. You are the true star in my eyes. Forever and always, I will love you.

Signed _____   Date _____

Poem: Long Live The Queen

Ave' Maria
Mary, how pure you are
Mary, how beautiful thou art
Mary, like a picture thou art poised
Mary Magdalene, I shall call you Mary
Your story is still a mystery
Wife of a joyful man
You did what no one ever could
Your bravery is unmatched
Eyes that reflect faith in the presence of defeat
You never did waver in sheer distress
Your King has died
Yet, here you stand
Purity?
Witchcraft?
Harlot?
Friend?
The story is unchanging, yet changes
We believe what is easiest to accept
We close our ears to soft melodies of truth
We couldn't dare rock the boat of fear
We're pleased with our King
Long live the King
Long live the King
May He live forever!

Mary
Mary
Mary?
Mary Magdalene
Does thou weep?
Does it offend that your name is a gamble?
Doest thou not know?
Did they not understand?
Thou stand as the hero
Fighting bravely beside your King
Weeping where you will
Smiling from cheek to cheek, seconds pass
You were tried in the fire
Your dreams made you ponder why
So different
Your soul whispered softly,
"Trust me, baby, life will unfold."
I look up to see you
I search the depth for a glimpse of you
You who the wind dost carry o'er
Bravely do you kneel
Confident that your children may carry on
Information
Stories
Lies
Cruelty
Truth
You lie in wait
Confident

Mary, the pure one
Mary, the holy mother

Mary, our sister
Mary Magdalene, the broken one
Hard life
Abuse
Your life is a gamble
They tore your silk dress
Your house lies in ruins
Your fish lay dead on the cold concrete
You are still so gentle and yet so firm
Harlot?
Strong?
Virgin?
Or not
To women who have walked the bitter streets
Who planted along the way
Daffodils
Rose bush
Orchids to brighten the glow
O, Oh womb of immortality!
Gates of the Ancient of Days
I drank from your Holy Grail
Eyes wide open
Long live the Queen!
Long live the Queen!
God save the Queen!

Join Me

For

Tea

A Special Brew: 1 Tsp of Transparency, 9 Slices of Wisdom & 1 Tsp of Courage

Conclusion

*S*ay this with me: "I strongly believe that God made me to be a success. I am not the horrible things in my past. I am not the abuse, and I choose not to become an abuser. I choose to give God my ashes with one hand and use the other hand to receive my beauty. My best days are fast approaching. My best self is quickly unfurling. I will learn to love myself and treat me the same way I long for others to. I am enough."

Now, go and live your best life to the extreme. God is to be found in everything you do, and everywhere your feet leave footprints in the sands of time.

Join Me

For

Tea

A Special Brew: 1 Tsp of Transparency, 9 Slices of Wisdom & 1 Tsp of Courage

About the Author

Roxanne Reid was born in the tropical paradise called Jamaica. She grew up in St. Catherine, and from the tender age of seven, she began exploring with paper and pens/pencils. When her grade six teacher affirmed that she had talent in writing, she finally believed. Her recent endeavours included graduating with honors—BA—specializing in English and Literature, starting her YouTube channel, "Soulfood Family," documenting poetry (included in this book), and creating an online mentoring workshop, "Lifestyle and Wellness Watch." She finds interest in playing golf, listening to binaural beats, reading across curriculum, and designing her wardrobe.

www.ingramcontent.com/pod-product-compliance
Lightning Source LLC
LaVergne TN
LVHW051154080426
835508LV00021B/2629